W9-AVC-680

W9-AVC-680

Editor: Penny Clarke
Consultant: Frank Meddens
Page make-up: Mark Whitchurch

FIONA MACDONALD
studied history at Cambridge University and the University of
East Anglia. She has taught in schools and adult education and
is the author of many children's books on historical subjects,
including *How Would You Survive in Aztec Times?* and *Keeping
Clean, A Very Peculiar History*, which won the Times
Educational Supplement's Senior Information Book award for
1995.

FRANK MEDDENS
was born in the Netherlands and subsequently studied at the
University of London. He has undertaken many research
projects in Peru as well as in Britain and Mexico. He has written
extensively on the Incas and other Peruvian cultures.

MARK BERGIN
was born in Hastings in 1961. He studied at Eastbourne College
of Art and now specializes in historical reconstructions. He lives
in Bexhill-on-Sea with his wife and their three children.

DAVID SALARIYA
studied illustration and printmaking in Dundee, Scotland. He
has created many books for publishers in the UK and overseas,
including the award-winning *Very Peculiar History* series. In
1989 he established The Salariya Book Company. He lives in
Brighton with his wife, the illustrator Shirley Willis, and their
son Jonathan.

Produced by
The SALARIYA BOOK CO. LTD
25 Marlborough Place
Brighton BN1 1UB

Published in 1998 by
Franklin Watts
96 Leonard Street
London EC2A 4RH

First American edition 1998 by
Franklin Watts
A Division of Grolier Publishing
Sherman Turnpike
Danbury, CT 06816

ISBN 0-531-14480 1
A copy of the Cataloging-in-Publication Data is available from
the Library of Congress

Printed in Singapore.

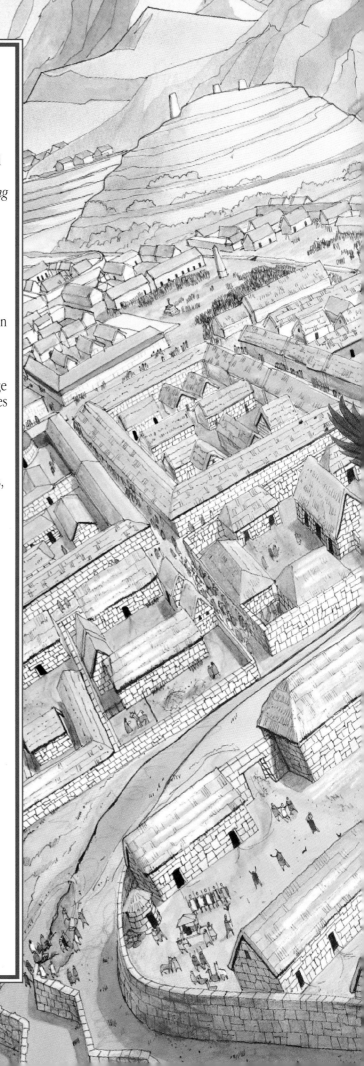

METROPOLIS

INCA TOWN

Written by Fiona Macdonald

Illustrated by Mark Bergin

Created and designed by David Salariya

W

FRANKLIN WATTS
A Division of Grolier Publishing
NEW YORK • LONDON • HONG KONG • SYDNEY
DANBURY, CONNECTICUT

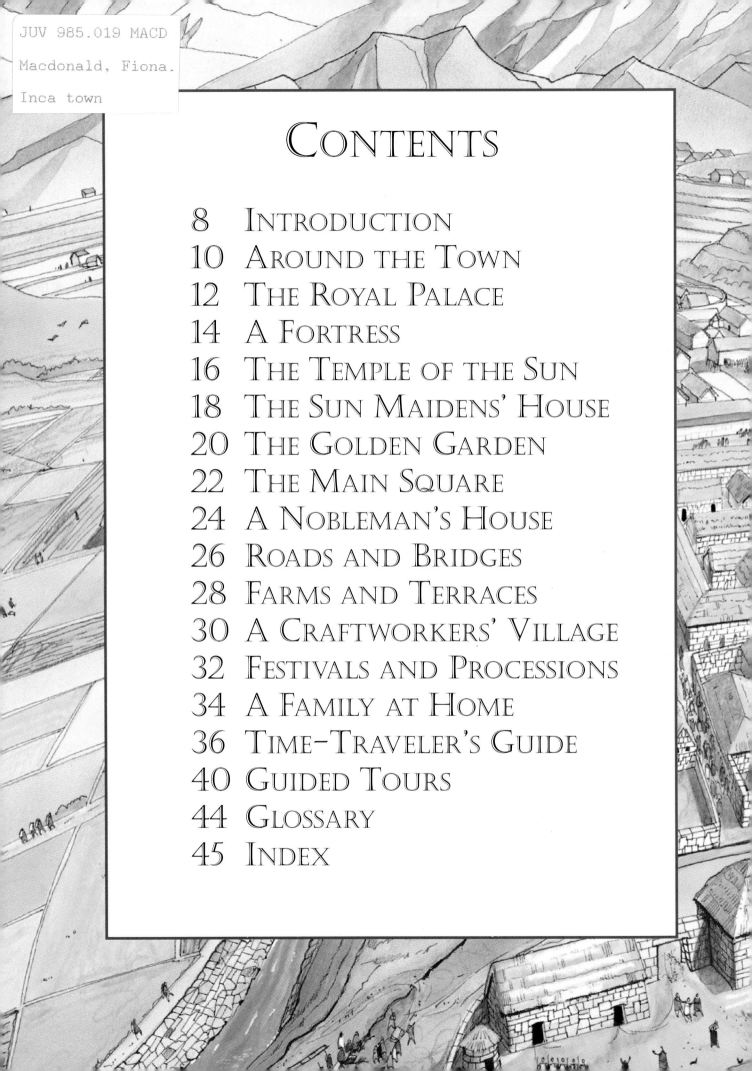

CONTENTS

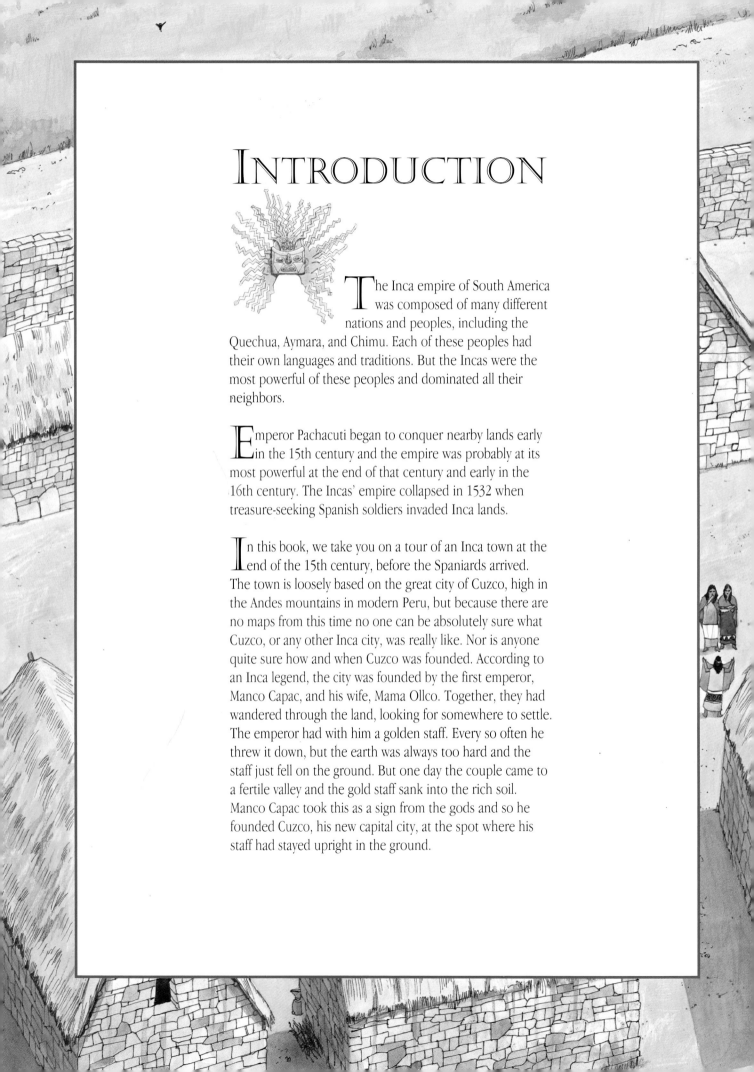

INTRODUCTION

The Inca empire of South America was composed of many different nations and peoples, including the Quechua, Aymara, and Chimu. Each of these peoples had their own languages and traditions. But the Incas were the most powerful of these peoples and dominated all their neighbors.

Emperor Pachacuti began to conquer nearby lands early in the 15th century and the empire was probably at its most powerful at the end of that century and early in the 16th century. The Incas' empire collapsed in 1532 when treasure-seeking Spanish soldiers invaded Inca lands.

In this book, we take you on a tour of an Inca town at the end of the 15th century, before the Spaniards arrived. The town is loosely based on the great city of Cuzco, high in the Andes mountains in modern Peru, but because there are no maps from this time no one can be absolutely sure what Cuzco, or any other Inca city, was really like. Nor is anyone quite sure how and when Cuzco was founded. According to an Inca legend, the city was founded by the first emperor, Manco Capac, and his wife, Mama Ollco. Together, they had wandered through the land, looking for somewhere to settle. The emperor had with him a golden staff. Every so often he threw it down, but the earth was always too hard and the staff just fell on the ground. But one day the couple came to a fertile valley and the gold staff sank into the rich soil. Manco Capac took this as a sign from the gods and so he founded Cuzco, his new capital city, at the spot where his staff had stayed upright in the ground.

AROUND THE TOWN

Golden Garden
These model plants and animals are very beautiful, but why are they in a garden? See pages 20 and 21.

Royal Palace
Who lives in this splendid palace? How should visitors behave if they are allowed inside? Find out more on pages 12 and 13.

A Family at Home
How do ordinary people live? What is life like for an Inca boy or girl? You'll find some answers on pages 34 and 35.

The Sun Maidens' House
Who are the Sun Maidens? What do they do? Investigate their lives on pages 18 and 19.

Festivals and Processions
What are these people carrying through the streets? Is that emperor alive or dead? Find out on pages 32 and 33.

A Nobleman's House
All sorts of important people live in Cuzco. What are their homes like? To find out, visit a noble Inca's house on pages 24 and 25.

The Temple of the Sun
Who is worshipped here? What will you see inside this holy place? Explore the great temple on pages 16 and 17.

A Craftworkers' Village
Who lives in this village, and what are they making? See some Inca craftworkers busy at work on pages 30 and 31.

Farms and Terraces
Why are the mountain slopes cut into terraces? What do these Inca farmers grow? Find out for yourself on pages 28 and 29.

The Main Square
This wide-open space is often full of people eating and drinking. But they are all usually very well behaved. Find out why on pages 22 and 23.

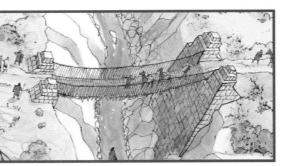

Roads and Bridges
What is the fastest way to get to Cuzco? Try one of these splendid roads. Travel like an Inca on pages 26 and 27.

A Fortress
What are these massive walls for? What is behind them? You can find out on pages 14 and 15.

THE ROYAL PALACE

V isitors to Cuzco are always very impressed by the royal palaces that stand at the city's heart. Whenever a new emperor comes to power he gives orders for a new palace to be built for himself and his wives, and fills it with completely new furniture. All the palaces are planned on the same design: a number of halls arranged around large courtyards, surrounded by strong stone walls. The emperor's own quarters, in the innermost part of the palace, are always closely guarded.

Anyone who wants to meet the emperor must take off their sandals and carry a small "burden" on their back. These are signs of respect. Visitors are also forbidden to look directly at the emperor; they must keep their eyes cast down all the time. Often, the emperor holds meetings while hidden behind a screen.

When they leave the palace, the Inca emperor and his wife travel in a litter, carried on the shoulders of specially chosen people.

According to legend, Manco Capac was the first Inca emperor. He reigned around AD 1200 and is revered by many Incas as the "Son of the Sun."

Inca emperors move conquered peoples far from their homelands. This is to make it difficult for them to rebel.

Inca laws are strict. First offenders are usually given a warning, but criminals caught several times are thrown into a pit with wild animals or hurled over a cliff.

Citizens pay their taxes in the form of labor, making or growing things from materials or seeds given by the state.

The emperor's treasury in Cuzco is full of silver and gold objects given by conquered princes or nobles seeking his favor.

A FORTRESS

When the emperor Pachacuti came to the throne in about 1438, the Incas' kingdom was quite small. But in less than 50 years they defeated all the neighboring peoples and dominated a huge area. The Incas certainly have an army, but their method of fighting (and gaining their empire) rarely involves major battles. Instead, the generals prefer to gain victories by negotiation and persuasion, backing this up with intimidation. Fighting is usually a last resort. Because of this, and also because they are so powerful, the Incas have not built many fortresses. Inside the few they have built are places to store emergency rations and a water supply that an enemy would find difficult to cut or poison.

Mitima, the system of moving conquered peoples to other parts of the empire, also helps to ensure peace.

Inca army commanders wear magnificent tunics, patterned with magic designs, and head-dresses made of feathers. They carry standards (decorated spears) which they use to give orders to their troops.

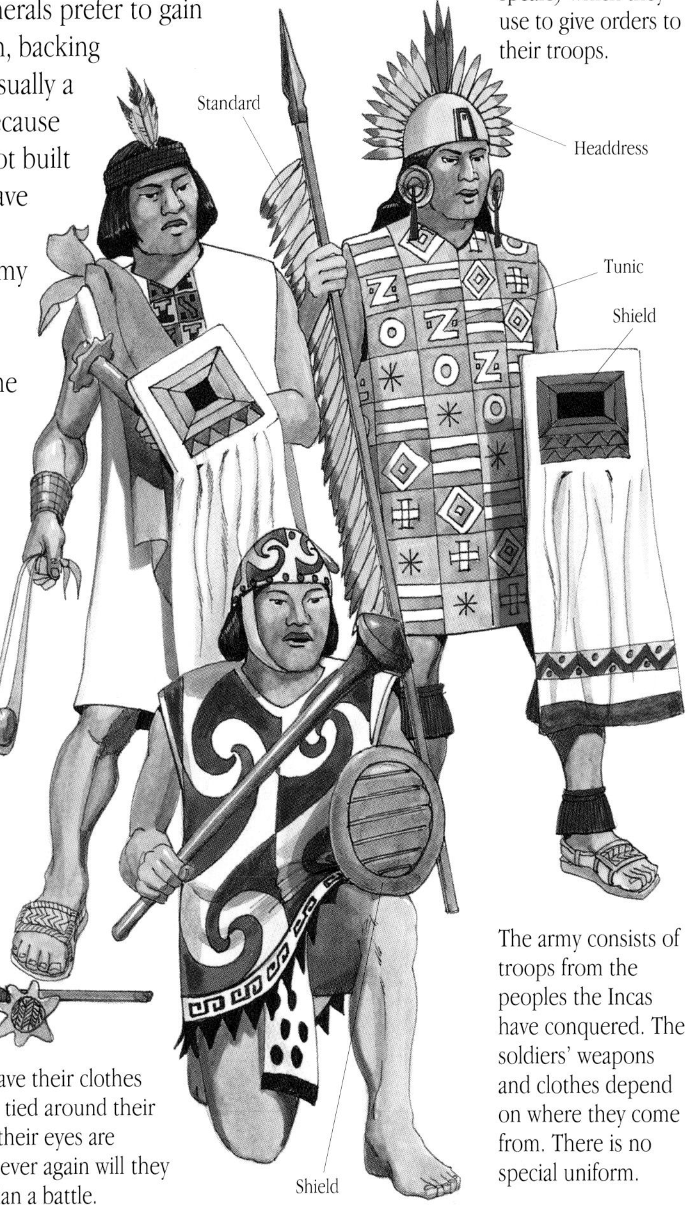

Standard

Headdress

Tunic

Shield

Slingshot

Some Inca soldiers use spears and clubs and wear padded cotton armor. Others fight with battle-axes and star-shaped stone "bolas."

Defeated enemies have their clothes removed and a rope tied around their necks. Occasionally their eyes are pulled out, so that never again will they be able to fight or plan a battle.

Shield

The army consists of troops from the peoples the Incas have conquered. The soldiers' weapons and clothes depend on where they come from. There is no special uniform.

THE TEMPLE OF THE SUN

The Nazcas, like the later Incas, made gold masks of their Sun god (right). Inca emperors claim that they are the sons of the Sun.

Sun's rays

The Coriancha, or Temple of the Sun, in the center of Cuzco, is famous throughout the empire as one of the great triumphs of Inca architecture. Like all the other important buildings, it is massive. The high walls are intended to awe visitors and show the power of the god – and his people (the Incas). Huge stones, carefully shaped and fitted together, form the lower part of the walls. The stone cutters' work is so precise that there is no need for mortar to hold the stones in place. The upper walls are made of adobe – sun-dried mud bricks. Inside are three separate stories, with places to worship, rooms for the priests and priestesses, and treasuries of sacred objects.

Hall of the Sun

Priests' houses and treasuries

High walls

High curved stone walls surround the Temple of the Sun and the Golden Garden (pages 20 and 21) next to it.

The Temple of the Sun is decorated with beautiful pictures setting out the Incas' view of the universe. In the center is Viracocha.

The Incas believe Viracocha is invisible. Around him are his children: the Sun and the Moon, and their off-spring, the Morning and Evening Stars. Below these stars are their children, Lord Earth and Lady Ocean. The Incas believe men and women are descended from them. In this painting the artists have shown rivers, mountains, animals, and plants – all created by Viracocha.

Viracocha

Sun
Moon
Morning Star
Evening Star

Summer stars
Winter stars

Lightning
Rainbow
Sea or lakes

Earth
Jaguar

Ruler

Holy sites
Ancestral tree

Pool
Man
Woman
Field

The Incas believe that their priests can see into the future by examining the entrails of a llama they sacrifice to the gods. They also say they can tell the outcome of a battle by looking at a dead llama's lungs.

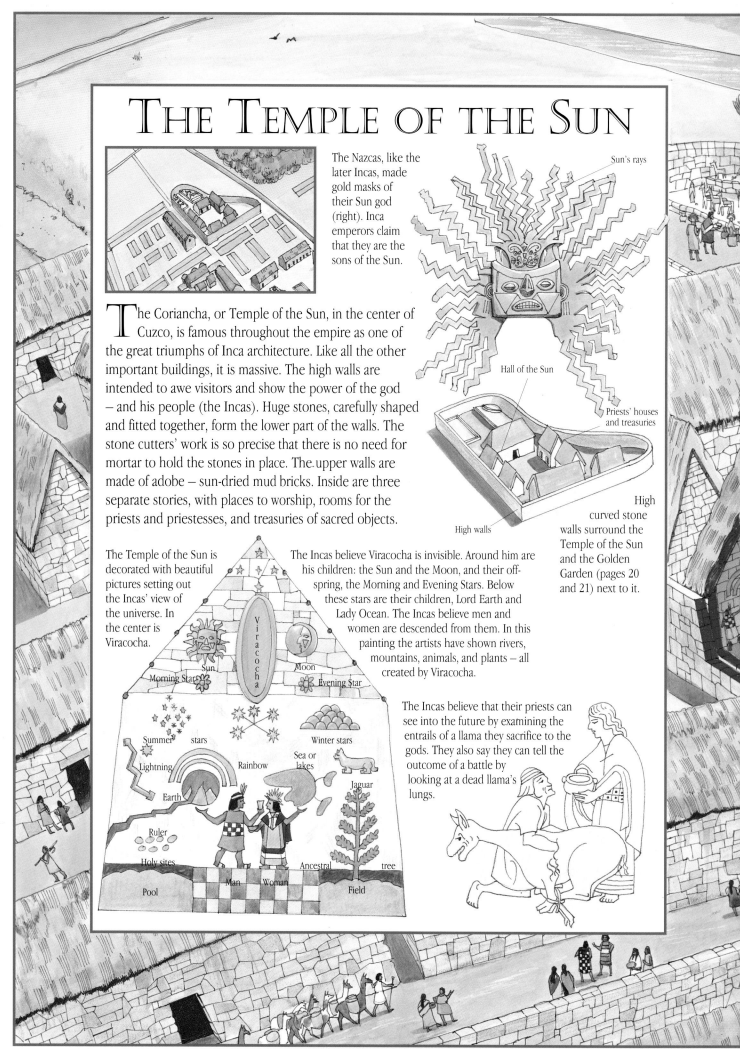

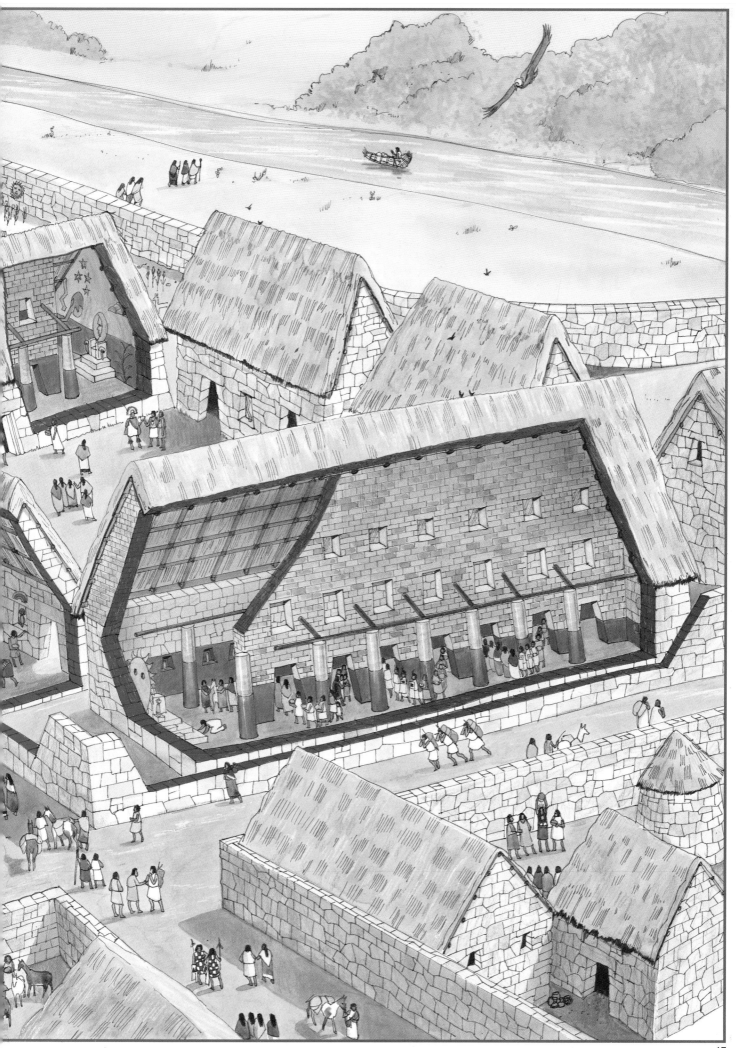

THE SUN MAIDENS' HOUSE

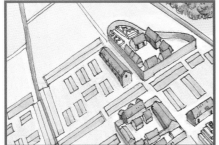

As well as serving in the Temple, the Sun Maidens spin thread and weave wonderful textiles for the emperor and his priests. It is said that they even weave robes from the incredibly fine hair of bats! Like other Inca women, the Sun Maidens also brew chicha, a special beer that is drunk on festival days.

Close to the great Sun Temple stands a large house. Like the emperor's palace, it has strong stone walls and a roof of thick straw thatch. It is guarded by well-armed soldiers. If any man – except the emperor or a few special priests – tries to enter he will be put to death. The house is well guarded because the Incas believe it is holy. It is the home of special priestesses, known as the Sun Maidens. It is their duty to help the priests who hold religious ceremonies in the Temple of the Sun. They spend their whole lives shut away here. The senior priestess is believed to be the wife of the Sun.

Girls are chosen to train as Sun Maidens when they are about ten years old. Royal officials visit all the villages to choose the prettiest and most talented girls.

The chosen girls are taken away to special schools (above) where they learn how to spin and weave the finest cloth (left). They also learn about religion and making chicha.

The Sun Maidens weave cloth from delicate threads: vicuna hair, feathers from rain forest birds, and strands of pure gold and silver.

Once trained, most girls become Sun Maidens, but a few face different fates. The emperor picks some as wives (he has hundreds), some are selected as wives of officials, and others are killed as sacrifices to the gods.

THE GOLDEN GARDEN

A wonderful garden stands next to the Temple of the Sun. It is unlike other gardens anywhere else in the world. It is full of beautiful animals, trees, and flowers – but they are all made of gold! The effect as the figures glitter and sparkle in the noonday sun is breathtaking. To the Incas, the display of gold and silver shows that this is holy ground. They regard gold as a very special metal. They often call it "the sweat of the Sun" and it is believed to have magical powers. It represents the Sun's life-giving force and so the power and authority of the Inca emperor, too. The Inca people also revere silver, calling it "the tears of the Moon." Like gold, it is said to have magical properties and represents the childbearing powers of the Coya, the Inca emperor's queen.

Ordinary people are not allowed to have gold – it is reserved for the royal family and the gods. Most gold and silver objects are made by hammering thin sheets of metal into shape.

Gold figure playing pan-pipes

This knife is even older than the Inca empire. Knives like it are used in all the Incas' religious rituals. The head-dress of the gold figure and his cloak are inlaid with semiprecious stones.

Lifelike models of people, animals, and plants are made out of gold and silver and given by important people as offerings to the gods.

Workers use furnaces of adobe (sun-dried clay) to smelt mineral ores to extract the gold, silver, and copper in them. They blow air down long cane pipes to raise the temperature of the fire high enough to melt the ore so it releases the metals.

THE MAIN SQUARE

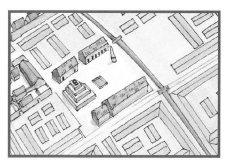

The first emperor, Manco Capac (right), with his wife, Mama Ollco. Cuzco, the Incas believed, stands in the valley where Manco Capac's golden staff at last sank into fertile soil.

This open space close to the center of Cuzco is the heart of the Inca empire. It is where the four main roads leading to the four "quarters" of the empire meet.

The main square is packed with people on holy days, especially at Inti Raymi, the supreme festival of the Sun, which takes place in June. The festival of Inti Raymi begins at dawn, when the emperor offers a cup of chicha to the Sun god (below). After the prayers, processions, and religious sacrifices are all over, the citizens hold a great feast in the huge public halls surrounding the square. They eat and drink in honor of the Sun. Vast amounts of chicha are consumed, and many people get drunk. However, bad behavior is very rare and getting drunk actually forms part of some special festivals.

This stone sundial stands on a special altar in the main square. The priests tell the time by measuring the shadow cast by the central pillar. At noon, when the sun is directly overhead, there is no shadow.

People believe that when the sundial's pillar casts no shadow it is because the Sun god has taken his seat on the top of the pillar.

The city is 11,550 feet (3,500 meters) up in the Andes and the white sand covering the main square has to be hauled up from the beaches along the coast! Llamas carry it in baskets slung across their backs.

Sixteen tall towers stand on the slopes of the mountains just outside the city. Like the sundial in the main square, they are used by priests and astronomers to observe the movements of the sun, moon, and stars across the sky.

A NOBLEMAN'S HOUSE

Lords from distant provinces and the sons of conquered kings are brought to Cuzco to learn Inca ways before being sent home to help run the empire.

Only Inca nobles and their wives are allowed to wear fine clothes, which are a sign of their rank.

Cuzco is a curious city, because few ordinary people live there. Most of its inhabitants are involved with running the empire: government officials, army commanders, royal servants, and high-ranking priests. All these important people need somewhere to live, so outside the center, which is reserved for royal and religious buildings, the streets are lined with fine houses that reflect their occupants' rank and power.

Like most Inca buildings, these noblemen's homes are simple in layout but very well built. The few windows are high up in the stone or adobe walls and the roofs are thatched. There is very little furniture. The Incas do not have chairs or beds, preferring to sit and sleep on piles of rugs and blankets on the floor.

High-ranking families like to decorate their homes with colorful rugs and blankets, woven from soft alpaca hair and dyed with leaves, berries, and crushed earth.

Tax collectors and government officials are sent from Cuzco to collect taxes and report on stocks of food in all the villages in the empire. Then they report back to the emperor. Records of all government business are kept on quipus – knotted, colored strings.

Senior officials, like this quipumayoc (quipu-reader), live in Cuzco, close to the emperor.

Building is laborious work. As much of the empire is in the Andes, hauling the stone is slow. Wheels are no use in the steep mountains!

Other important people, like master masons and building overseers, also live in Cuzco.

ROADS AND BRIDGES

The Inca empire is vast. It stretches for almost 2,400 miles (4,000 kilometers) from north to south. The Inca emperors need good roads if they are to run their empire efficiently. Sometimes, they need to march an army long distances to put down a rebellion; sometimes they must send urgent messages to government officials a long way away. To meet these needs, Inca emperors have ordered the building of many roads and bridges throughout the empire.

They have also built tambos, rest houses for people traveling on government business to use. In the Atacama Desert, which is on the coast, the winds often blow sand across the roads. To prevent travelers getting lost, yard-high piles of stones are placed on each side of the road every 66 feet (20 meters). Inca roads measure about 3 feet (0.9 meters) wide. Wherever possible they are straight, but roads in the Andes follow a zigzag course because that is the best way to get over the mountain slopes. Where the mountain sides are particularly steep, the road is a series of steps cut into the rock.

So that messages reach their destinations quickly, the government has teams of relay runners, called chasquis, on duty 24 hours a day, to carry messages or bundles of quipus to and from Cuzco. Chasquis wait in shelters beside the road, ready to run. Each team serves for 15 days and can cover about 132 miles (220 kilometers) in a day.

Inca roads are paved with stone, fitted together to form a level surface. Keeping roads in good repair (below) is part of the tax paid by people living nearby.

People use tumplines – wide bands of fabric across their foreheads and over their shoulders – to carry big loads.

Llamas are used as pack animals to carry heavy loads because they are strong and surefooted. Officials lead trains of them along the roads in and out of Cuzco.

Suspension bridges are made of grasses, vines, or twigs twisted into ropes (top). The thickest are 16 in (40 cm) in diameter. A bridge is made of five thick ropes. Three are joined by thinner ones to form the walkway; the other two are handrails.

FARMS AND TERRACES

The countryside surrounding Cuzco is not an easy place to live. It is about 11,200 feet (3,500 meters) above sea level, and can get very cold. Yet the soil is fertile, there is rain in summer, and crops like potatoes, quinoa, and oca can grow well if they are fertilized with llama manure. Because the valley sides are so steep, they are cut into narrow terraces, like giant steps around the mountainsides.

Farming is organized by the government. Villagers who work in the fields receive a house and a food allowance, instead of wages. The rest of the food they produce is taken to Cuzco to feed the citizens there, or else stored in granaries for emergencies – such as crop failure or even a volcanic eruption, for many Andean mountains are active volcanoes.

Potatoes can be grown at higher altitudes than some of the Inca farmers' other crops. Peppers and avocados, for example, need warmer temperatures. Other foods include peanuts, gourd seeds, and broad, or lima, beans. The tubers (swollen roots) of the yucca plant (left) are another popular food. The tubers are boiled or roasted.

Gourd seeds

Peanuts

Corn grains and beans

Corn (below) is the main food. It can be toasted until crisp, heated to make popcorn, or boiled to a mush.

Grain is stored in stone granaries thatched with reeds or dried grass.

Women cook in clay pots on small clay stoves that burn wood or dried llama dung. On festival days, they grind corn into flour to make porridge, small cakes, or dumplings.

Farmers channel water from mountain streams to irrigate their fields. This is essential on the dry western slopes if they are to have good harvests.

Because of its size, the empire's climate varies enormously. Rain comes from the east and falls on the tropical lowlands and eastern mountain slopes. The western mountain slopes and west coast are dry. The snow-covered mountains are too high and cold for anyone to live there, and the "puna" (high plateau) is very windswept.

West   East

Rain

Sea

Mountains

Puna – high plains

Coastal desert

Wet lowlands

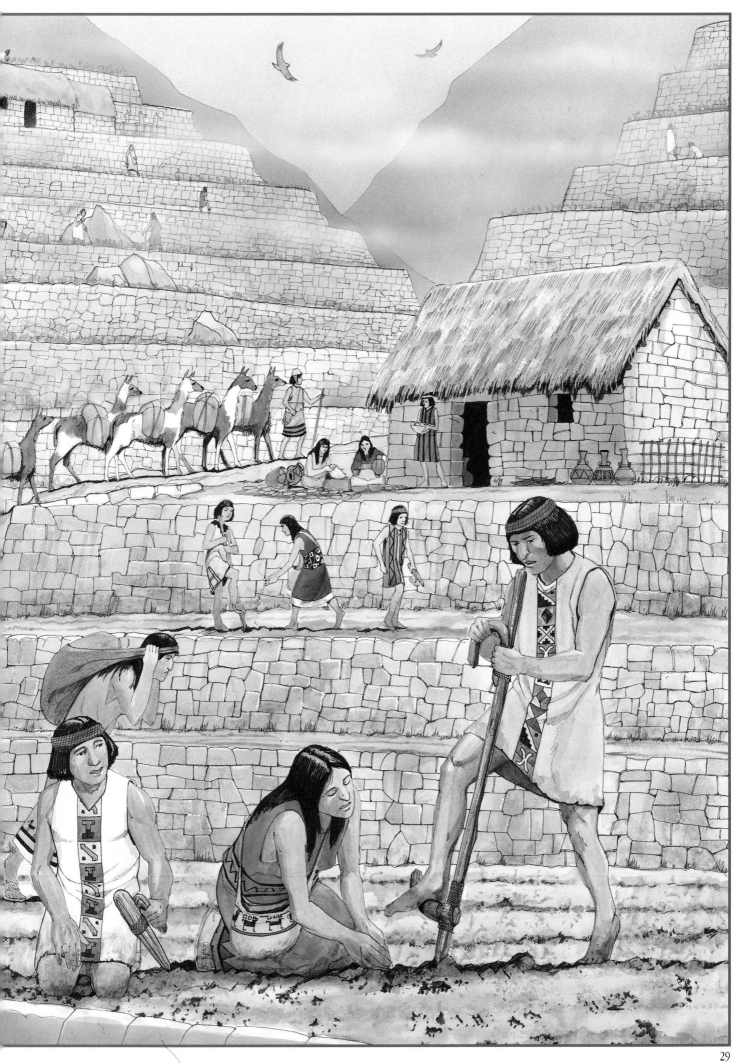

A Craftworkers' Village

To prepare clay for making pottery, the craftsmen knead it with their feet, then roll it into sausage-shaped strips called "bolos." Then the clay is ready to be used.

A few particularly skilled craftworkers, such as the metalworkers from Chimu, live in their own special quarters in Cuzco. But in general, it is the responsibility of certain villages with a reputation for producing high quality goods to supply items such as cloth, gold jewelry, and pottery as a way of paying their taxes. Spinning is one of the first craft skills that children learn.

Like all ordinary Inca people, craftworkers live in simple village homes, usually with just one room heated by a smoky cooking stove. The family's few possessions are hung from wooden pegs, or put in baskets and clay jars stacked on the floor. Often, groups of close relations live in houses built around a courtyard.

Inca potters are renowned for creating vessels in many fantastic shapes. The designs are often based on plants and animals and the potter adds human hands and faces. Then geometric decorations are carefully painted onto each pot.

Inca potters do not use a wheel. Instead they mold and shape everything by hand. Large plain pots are made by coiling lengths of clay round and round, gradually building up the sides of the pot. Finally the pots are smoothed inside and out.

Some craftsmen specialize in carving stone (below and below right). It is slow work carving these artifacts from the hard volcanic stone. The patterns decorating the containers and bowls are mostly of animals and plants.

The cat was carved by craftsmen 2,000 years before the Incas came to power. It is now a treasured heirloom.

All kinds of things are carved from wood. (Left to right): Beaker (called a "kero"), pin (used to fasten cloaks), a small figure, and a spoon.

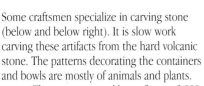

FESTIVALS AND PROCESSIONS

It is an honor to be chosen as a sacrifice to the gods. The chosen one is dressed in her finest clothes (right) and given a magnificent headdress as a sign of respect to the gods. Afterwards she will be buried in a tomb cut out of the rock (below). The body is put in a crouching position, like a baby in the womb. This is a symbol that she will be reborn. Pots and bowls, for her afterlife, are put in the tomb, too.

If you stay long in Cuzco, you will almost certainly see one of the city's many religious festivals. These are usually accompanied by music, singing, and dancing, and sometimes by processions, when religious treasures are carried through the streets of Cuzco. The Incas believe that displaying their sacred objects in this way encourages the gods to protect them, and reassures the citizens that all is well. At the most important festivals, the mummified bodies of dead emperors are dressed in fine clothes and join the parade through the streets.

The bodies of some important officials are wrapped in cloth and placed in stone tower tombs called chulpas. Sometimes a mask of clay or precious metal is put over the face before the body is put in the tomb. Ordinary people are put in crevices in the rocks.

Beakers and bowls to bury with the dead.

Children are often killed as offerings to the gods, to bring good luck and prevent disasters. Little statues like this are usually placed beside sacrificed girls and boys.

When an emperor dies, some of his servants and wives are killed to keep him company in the next world. They are given lots of chicha to calm their fears before they die.

A FAMILY AT HOME

Y ou will not see any ordinary family homes in Cuzco because ordinary people are not allowed to live there. However, if you have a chance to travel in the Inca empire you will see villages where ordinary people live. You will find their homes are very similar to the houses in the craft-workers' village: small, single-story buildings with thatched roofs. There is usually only one room, although sometimes a family will hang up blankets or skins to divide the room into several smaller areas.

Everyone has to work hard to help support the family, even small children. Whatever the family produces, whether it is crops or craft goods, is assessed for tax, which is paid in food or goods. Government officials take away the tax payments to be stored by the state. But, if a family falls on hard times, perhaps because their crops fail or they have a serious illness or accident, the government will give them food and clothing from these stores.

Everyone gets married, usually in their teens. The couple's parents often arrange the marriage, which must be approved by government officials at a special ceremony held once a year. Only nobles can have more than one wife, but even they must have the emperor's permission.

Boys learn how to aim and kill prey with a slingshot (right). This is a hard stone thrown from a cloth or leather sling. As well as being a good hunting weapon, slingshots are used in fighting.

Families who live close to the coast, or beside one of Peru's great lakes, make their living from fishing and collecting shells. Boys are taught how to build and sail reed boats and rafts, and how to catch fish in big nets, woven from cotton (below right).

After their day's work fishing, trapping birds in nets or looking after the family's herds of animals on the mountainside, boys play boardgames and games with a whip and spinning top (left).

Inca girls learn how to prepare food, cook, clean, collect firewood and light fires, and run a household. Learning to spin thread from llama and alpaca wool is particularly important. The long, silky wool from alpacas is highly prized, and to get the wool the women and girls in a family regularly comb the animals.

In spite of all the chores, there is usually time to play with the family's guinea pigs (above) or wooden or terra-cotta dolls.

Time-Traveler's Guide

When to Travel

The city of Cuzco is south of the Equator, so you'll need to remember that local "winter" and "summer" seasons may not be the same as those you are used to at home. In the Inca highlands, "summer" runs from December to March, while "winter" lasts from April to November. There is no real spring or autumn. In terms of temperature, it will not matter very much what time of year you choose to travel. At 10,923 feet (3,310 meters) above sea level, Cuzco is so high that it never gets really hot in the summer. But although temperatures are much the same year-round, you will notice a big difference between the day and night temperatures. During the day it can reach 68°F (20°C), but at night, especially in June, July, and August, temperatures can drop to below freezing.

Nor is there very much rain. Only about 28.6 inches (715 millimeters) fall in Cuzco each year, mostly in winter. Summer is the driest season and weeks can pass without any rain and dust can be a problem.

What to Wear

Take a tip from the locals and wear several layers of warm clothing. Otherwise the icy winds sweeping down from the Andes' snow-covered peaks will chill you to the bone.

Inca clothes are colorful and warm. Men wear loose tunics, about knee-length, with a long cloak on top. They cover their heads with wool caps and wear leather or (more usually) woven grass sandals on their feet. Women wear ankle-length tunics, with a wide shawl pinned over their shoulders. For extra warmth they wear a long cloak, too. They do not wear hats; instead, they pull their cloaks or shawls over their heads. Like the men, they wear grass sandals, or else slippers made of felted wool.

Many visitors find the thin highland air very harsh on their skin. Humidity is low and the strong mountain winds are very drying, so windburn can be more of a problem than sunburn. In the tropical areas it is much hotter, and also more humid, and prickly heat is a danger, as well as sunburn.

What to Eat

Food is plain and simple, and usually vegetarian. The food you will eat will depend on where you go. In the lowlands there is more variety than in the highlands. Besides corn, the staple food, you will be offered chillis, pumpkins, beans, sweet potatoes, peanuts, avocados, tomatoes, and cassava. These are usually made into stews. In highland regions, your meals will be based on potatoes, with quinoa and other edible seeds stewed to make porridge. On special occasions, meat will be served – probably guinea pig, llama, alpaca, or wild deer. Most villagers keep guinea pigs in their homes. They also breed ducks, which are good roasted. Fish is common on the coast and by the lakes. Dog meat is sometimes available. Chicha is the most common drink. Don't think about how it is made if you are squeamish – women chew raw corn kernels to soften them and spit the pulp into clay jars. When there is enough pulp it is mixed with water, then left to ferment.

TIME-TRAVELER'S GUIDE

LOCAL LANGUAGES

The people you meet in Cuzco will mostly speak Quechua, the South American language spoken by the first Inca leaders, like Manco Capac, and by the people they ruled. You may also meet people from lands conquered by the Incas who will speak different local languages, but if they have lived in Cuzco for a long while, or have official positions, they will probably speak Quechua, as well as their own language.

Quechua follows certain clear rules. Once you have mastered them you should be able to make yourself understood reasonably easily.

Here are a few Quechua words. "Huaca" means "holy," you will find that there are many holy things and holy places throughout the Inca empire, all of which you must treat respectfully. "Charqui" means "dried meat" – drying is the most usual way of preserving things in this part of the world. And did you know that the name "Cuzco" means "navel"? The Incas called their capital this because they believed it was the center of the world.

A HEAD FOR HEIGHTS?

As you know, Cuzco is very high above sea level. To spend a happy and healthy time there you need to develop a head for heights. This means two different things. First, you will have to get used to dizzying mountain slopes, with terraced fields and steep, narrow tracks. You will also have to cope with rope bridges, swaying 198 feet (60 meters) or more above rocky mountain gorges and rushing mountain torrents. You may even have to be hauled across rivers in a basket hanging from a rope – the Inca way to cross a river if there is not enough traffic to justify building a bridge.

Second, you must take things very gently when you first arrive. There is much less oxygen at high altitudes than at sea level, because the mountain air is so thin. However, you can get "altitude sickness" at lower levels than Cuzco. If you get a headache, or chest pains or feel dizzy and short of breath, rest for a few days. Altitude sickness is not a problem for the Incas because their bodies have adapted to the thin air.

ACCIDENTS & FIRST AID

Accidents will happen even on the best organized visit. There are Inca doctors who perform some very risky operations, such as trepanning – cutting holes in the skull. Avoid these, except in absolute emergencies! But other doctors make useful medicines from herbs and crushed rocks. For example, they use sap from pepper plants as a soothing antiseptic to help heal wounds, yucca (cassava) leaves to help aching joints, and powdered clay to ease gout. These remedies have been tried and tested for centuries and may work very well; they are unlikely to do you any harm although they may not do you much good. But don't try making your own medicines from unknown plants – they might make you sick, or even kill you.

You will see local people chewing coca leaves. They say the leaves, which contain cocaine, help them withstand hunger, exhaustion, and cold, but you will not be there long enough to get cold, hungry, or exhausted – unless you do too much sightseeing!

37

TIME-TRAVELER'S GUIDE

WHAT TO BARTER

BE PREPARED

STAYING OUT OF TROUBLE

It will be difficult to buy souvenirs of your visit because officially there is no private trade anywhere within the Inca empire. The people do not have coins or any other sort of currency, and all business dealings are controlled by the state. Any private trading that takes place is usually a form of bartering between networks of relatives living in different areas. Each area is likely to have different resources, such as food, so people in one area contact people in another area to see if they would like to exchange goods between the two areas. These networks of relatives are strengthened and often extended by the Incas' system of arranged marriages.

Most people just barter anything they have handy, but there are a few groups that specialize in a particular trade. The Chincha, for example, get "mullu," a type of shell, from neighboring people who live on the coast of the Pacific Ocean north of the Inca empire (modern Ecuador). Then the Chincha barter the shells for other goods.

Be sure that you take enough valuable things with you to barter for food, accommodation, and transportation. You may find Inca families very generous, but you must be prepared to be self-sufficient. Inca society is so well organized that it is almost impossible for outsiders to "fit in." Inca government may seem harsh, but it brings many benefits, looking after citizens from the cradle to the grave.

Each family is allowed to own a certain amount of land to grow its food. The more children a family has, the more land it is given. If a woman's husband dies, officials arrange for her family's land to be farmed for her. People who are old, sick, or disabled are fed, clothed, and housed by the state. In return for this care, Inca people have to pay taxes in labor, or work for the state for a certain number of days a year. Even old and disabled people must contribute, for example, by removing seeds from the bolls of fluffy cotton heads, keeping an eye on babies, or picking lice from children and animals.

Inca laws are very strict, and punishments are harsh. The most serious offences are punished by death. Remember, too, that everyone's actions are watched by government officials – and they are everywhere! As a result, you may find people rather nervous about talking to such an obvious stranger. Do not ask any Inca people you meet to do anything unlawful – and try not to break any Inca laws yourself!

The greatest crimes are treason and disobedience to the emperor. Stealing from temples, fields, state granaries, and tambos are serious offenses, too. Inca officials also take a very dim view of people who vandalize roads and bridges, and of people working for the state who cheat or fail to do their duty. There are no prisons in the Inca empire – someone accused of a serious crime will be seized by soldiers and kept under armed guard. Courts are run by government officials. They may order suspects to be tortured, to make them confess to their crimes – whether they are guilty or not.

TIME-TRAVELER'S GUIDE

A YEAR OF FESTIVALS

The Inca year has twelve lunar months of 28 days. Each month has its own special festivals. All are fascinating to observe, but remember, they are sacred occasions for the Inca people, so treat them with respect. Most of the festivals are linked to important stages in the farming year – preparing the soil, planting seeds, and the harvest – and are designed to encourage the sun to shine, the rains to fall, and the plants and animals to grow.

The cycle of festivals begins in September. The main festival that month is Cituay Raymi. It is to cleanse Cuzco of all disease and bad things. So you, together with anyone with a physical defect and all dogs, will have to leave the city. The ashes of a ritual fire are taken by four bands of warriors and thrown into different rivers. The ashes, together with everything bad that they symbolize, will be carried by the rivers to the sea.

In October, after all the crops have been sown, comes Uma Raymi. Sacrifices are made to the gods to ask them for rain for the newly planted crops.

THROUGH THE YEAR

December is an exciting month for boys. At the festival of Capac Raymi they are initiated into manhood and become warriors. They can now own llamas and wear plugs in their earlobes like the other adult men. To ensure a good rainfall for the crops, the young men hold a mock battle in the main square in January.

Then, in February, to encourage the gods to help the crops to ripen, guinea pigs and wood are offered at Hatun Pucuy. Llamas and alpaca, which are so important to the Inca way of life, have a special festival in April. Everyone hopes that it will ensure the animals remain healthy and have many young. The following month many llamas are sacrificed to celebrate the corn harvest in the festival of Hatun Cuzqui. A good harvest means there will be plenty to eat until the next harvest.

In July the importance of irrigation to Inca farming is celebrated in Cahuarquis. Then, in August, the farming year begins again with Yapaquiz, the celebration of the sowing of the new year's corn seed.

VISITING A SHRINE

The Incas have many places and objects that they regard as sacred. They call these holy things "huacas," and believe they are inhabited by a spirit that has the power to help people or to cause terrible harm.

You will see all kinds of huacas as you travel around the city and the country – great temples, strangely shaped rocks or caves, majestic mountain peaks, ancient burial grounds, and springs of fresh water by the side of the road. The Incas believe that invisible, holy lines link these places, so they always approach a huaca with respect, in case they annoy the sacred spirit that lives there. For the same reason, they always make an offering when they visit one. You should do the same, to avoid causing alarm or giving offense to the gods.

Offerings need not be large or valuable. The rich give gold and silver items, or lengths of cloth, but some corn or fruit would do. The very poorest villagers may offer just one or two of their eyelashes. The Incas believe it is the thought that is important!

GUIDED TOURS

THE MAIN SQUARE

Cuzco is the center of the Inca empire and the main square is the center of Cuzco, so that's the obvious place to start your first tour of the city!

As you stand in the square and look at all the handsome stone buildings around you, it is difficult to realize that all the development you see is really quite new.

Until about 500 years ago, Cuzco was a large, rambling, rather ramshackle town on the edge of a misty swamp. According to tradition, things changed around 1440, in the reign of the emperor Pachacuti. He is believed to have decided to rebuild Cuzco. Certainly, the magnificent capital city you are about to explore is quite unlike that earlier town on the edge of the swamp, with all the damp, cold and diseases associated with such sites. Now Cuzco is a showplace for Inca craft skills, and a symbol of the Inca empire's power.

The reason for moving the city lay deep within the Incas' religious beliefs, which are difficult for visitors to learn about. But one of the reasons was the Incas' belief that Cuzco was the navel – the absolute center – of the whole world. All the empire's

towns and villages were built within a series of magical (but invisible) lines. Building within these lines ensured good luck. There were, however, doubts about the position of Cuzco. So, after many sacrifices to the gods and long discussions with the senior priests, it was decided to move the city.

As a result, the center of the city was moved north, so that the main square in which you are now standing was at the center of all the empire's magical, invisible lines. Whether it was Pachacuti or another emperor who decided on the move does not really matter, the importance of Cuzco shows that the decision and choice of position were right – otherwise the empire would not have

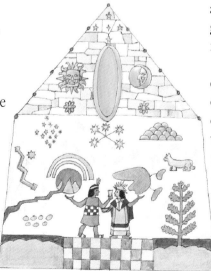

become so powerful.

The Inca name for the main square is Huacaypata. It is a vast open space covering about 10 acres (4 hectares), and is where many of the great religious ceremonies are staged. In the middle is a stone platform where the emperor stands to perform his ritual duties.

If you are lucky enough to be visiting Cuzco on the first day of the month you'll find the square packed with people, because a special ceremony is taking place. The emperor and his courtiers have come to inspect 100 specially chosen llamas and then to watch them being led four times in a circle around images of the most important gods. The high priest then dedicates the llamas to Viracocha and shares them out among 30 high-ranking government officials. Each receives three or four llamas.

After the ceremony is over, wait for the crowds to clear before starting your exploration of the city. As you wait, have a look at the halls and palaces around the square. No one will mind if you pause to look at them, but take care not to linger too long – it might cause suspicious glances in your direction.

GUIDED TOURS

THE CITY CENTER

One of the first things you'll notice about Cuzco is just how crowded the city center is, and how closely packed the buildings are.

The central area of city, where you'll find all the important buildings, is about 6,600 feet (2,000 meters) long by 1,980 feet (600 meters) wide. There are well over 4,000 buildings, as well as two enormous squares. Probably about 300,000 people live in the city and the nearby villages.

Most visitors are also usually overwhelmed at just how huge and well built everything is. Temples, palaces, and nobles' houses tower high above the narrow streets. It's like walking through a city built for giants!

Visitors with an interest in architectural technology always find the way in which the buildings have been constructed fascinating – and usually quite different from anything they have seen before. Cuzco is in an earthquake zone – you may experience the occasional tremor during your stay – and buildings made in the normal way, using mortar to hold the stones or bricks together, would be very dangerous. They would simply collapse

on the inhabitants everytime there was an earthquake or tremor. But Cuzco's stone-masons build using a different technique – they do not use mortar. Instead, each block is carefully shaped (everything is done by hand) to fit neatly and tightly against the neighboring stones and the top of each course (layer) of stonework is slightly hollowed. When the earth shakes, all the stones shift against one another but stay in place, and the building does not fall down. So, if you are out and about when there is a tremor, don't worry, you won't be killed or injured by falling buildings!

When you have finished exploring the main square make your way to the southwest corner. There you will find a

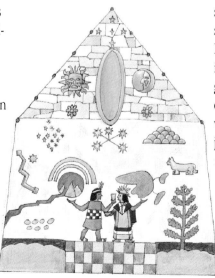

steep flight of steps. Climb down them and you will come to another square. Although smaller than Huacaypata, it is still very large. This square is called Cusipata, "Place of Joy" and is used for feasts and other social gatherings. There are halls along the sides, where citizens meet to eat and drink on festival days. If you are here while a festival is taking place, you will be able to join the crowds out enjoying themselves.

When you've had a look around, return to the flight of steps you reached it by. Climb back up the steps into the main square and then turn right. A short walk will bring you to the house where the Sun Maidens live. You will not be able to see inside, nor will you see any sign of them, but there is nothing to stop you from admiring the fine stonework of the strong walls. Like most buildings in Cuzco, it is constructed from a close-grained gray stone, hewn from quarries in the Andes. In one wall there is a fine example of just how skillful the Inca stone-masons are: Look for the stone that has been so carefully shaped and fitted among the others that it has twelve sides. No wonder the city's buildings withstand earthquakes!

GUIDED TOURS

TOURING THE EMPIRE

As you continue your walk through the streets, keep well clear of the armed guards outside the royal palaces nearby.

If you continue walking in a southeasterly direction you will soon see ahead of you a building decorated with strips of glittering gold. This is the Coriancha, the Temple of the Sun. It is built of a special deep red stone that is reserved for the most important temples. It is the most famous huaca (holy place) in the empire because it is so close to where all the magic, invisible lines meet. So you must be sure to behave very respectfully as you pass it – walk slowly and if you are with anyone keep your voices down.

The beautiful Golden Garden stands next door. Ask the gatekeepers whether it would be possible for you to have a peep through the gates. Only the emperor and nobility are allowed into the Coriancha and the Golden Garden – and you are certainly not one of them!

Nearby you will be able to see another of the Incas' great engineering achievements, also said to have been ordered by Pachacuti – two rivers that flow in deep stone channels on either side of the city's center. These channels were built to carry away melting snow from the high mountain slopes, as well as the water that used to collect in the nearby marsh. That marsh is now completely drained. It is amazing to think that these two neat, well-controlled rivers are part of a mighty natural water system that eventually flows into the Amazon River and reaches the sea on the far side of South America, off the coast of Brazil!

As you explore, it is worth remembering that the stone channels built to contain the two rivers mark the boundary of the city center. All Cuzco's most important buildings, like the temples and the royal palaces, stand between them. Houses and barns are outside.

If you want to see more of the empire than just the capital, you will need to do some careful organization. The government controls the lives of all the citizens so firmly that the idea of anyone wanting – or having the time – to travel just to please themselves is one you'll have difficulty explaining; it is something that does not happen in the lives of ordinary people. Your best hope of seeing more of the empire is to join a group of officials traveling on government business. At least they are used to traveling as part of their work, although they too probably won't understand the idea of traveling for its own sake.

Before deciding where to go, barter something in exchange for a drink or a snack to eat. If you can find somewhere to do this close to one of the government buildings you might be able to discover from one of the guards if officials are likely to be traveling on business to one of the four quarters into which the Inca empire is divided.

Chinchaysuyu is in the north, Antisuyu is in the east, Cuntisuyu is in the southwest, and Collasuyu is in the far south. The road to each quarter starts at the main square, so that could be another source of information.

Chinchaysuyu stretches from the Pacific coast to the foothills of the Andes. It is mostly dry, semidesert grassland, broken by rocky outcrops and deep river valleys carrying icy torrents of melted snow. Only about 10 percent of the land is suitable for farming, but the best corn in the entire empire is grown here. The wonderful statues that you glimpsed in the Golden Garden were made by the Chimu who live in this quarter.

If you join a party going to Antisuyu you will need many different clothes, for this quarter includes areas of great extremes – from cold high mountain ranges to warm wet lowlands through which the Amazon River flows. This variety makes the quarter one of the most interesting areas of the empire to visit. You will see many different crops being grown on the terraced hillsides. As well as corn, cotton, and coca (both valuable crops) are grown here. Much of the lowland is covered by rain forest. As well as being an excellent source of food, particularly fruit, the rain forest is home to many

animals and birds. If you are in Cuzco for one of the festivals, you are likely to see the emperor and his nobles wearing magnificent ceremonial headdresses. The feathers from which they are made come from the rain forest in Antisuyu.

Cuntisuyu, which is the smallest quarter, is not such an interesting region. Running along the Pacific coast to the southwest of Cuzco, much of it is desert and so extremely dry and inhospitable for anyone not used to living there. Local people say that sometimes it does not rain for hundreds of years at a time! As you can imagine, farming is almost impossible in such a climate, but the people survive by fishing, because the waters of the sea

close to the coast are chilled by an ocean current which teems with fish. Although the area is largely desert, it is not always hot and dry. In winter the cold seawater causes dense fogs. These fogs envelop the land along the coast, providing enough moisture to germinate seeds lying dormant in the ground. For a few weeks the land is carpeted with grass and flowering plants. Herds of wild guanaco come down from the mountains to graze and local people kill them for meat and skins. When the fogs clear, at the beginning of spring, the plants wither as the ground dries out and becomes desert once again.

Collasuyu is mostly high flat grassland, suitable only for grazing llama and alpaca. Lake Titicaca is in this quarter. The lake, one of the world's largest and highest expanses of fresh water, provides fish for the Aymara people who live by it. They also grow potatoes and quinoa, one of the few grains that will grow in the harsh conditions. The Aymara, who were one of the first nations conquered by the Incas, sail on the lake in boats they make from reeds. Barter something and you could have a sail too!

Glossary

Adobe Sundried mud bricks.

Alloy A mixture of several different metals.

Alpaca A small mountain animal, related to camels. Bred by the Incas for its fine wool.

Altitude sickness A disease caused by lack of oxygen; common among travelers to high mountain regions.

Barter To "buy" and "sell" goods by exchanging them for items of a similar value.

Bola An Inca weapon, consisting of a heavy stone or star-shaped lump of metal attached to a rope.

Bolls Fluffy seed pods of the cotton plant.

Causeways Roads raised above the surrounding land on banks of earth.

Chasqui [Chas-key] A runner who carried government messages.

Chicha Inca beer, brewed from corn.

Coca A small evergreen bush. Its leaves contain the source of the drug cocaine. Inca people chewed coca to help them cope with hunger and exhaustion.

Entrails The internal organs of an animal – heart, lungs, stomach etc.

Felt A wool fabric that has been boiled until it turns into a solid mass.

Guanaco [Goo-an-na-ko] A wild animal, similar to a llama, but larger. Hunted by the Incas for its meat.

Huaca [Wa-ca] A holy place.

Kero [Key-row] A tall, curved beaker, usually made of wood.

Litter A portable bed.

Llama A mountain animal, related to camels. It was bred to carry heavy loads along mountain tracks, and for its wool. Llamas were also sacrificed to the gods.

Mitima The Inca system of moving defeated people away from their homelands and settling them elsewhere, as a way of controlling them and preventing rebellions.

Puma A wild mountain animal of the cat family, like a leopard.

Puna A high, open grasslands in between mountain ranges.

Quechua [Kech-oo-ah] The language of the Inca people. It is still spoken by many people in South America today.

Quinoa [Key-no-ah] A mountain plant grown for its seeds, which were cooked to make porridge.

Quipu [Key-poo] A record of business, made of bundles of colored, knotted string.

Tambo A resting place beside roads for Inca government officials and other travelers.

Trepanning Cutting holes in the skull. A medical technique, designed to release evil spirits that caused madness and pain.

Tribute Goods paid as taxes by conquered peoples.

Tumplines Broad bands of fabric that pass across the forehead and over the shoulders, used for carrying heavy loads.

Vicuna [Vee-coo-nya] Wild animal like a llama, but smaller. Prized for its fine wool.

INDEX

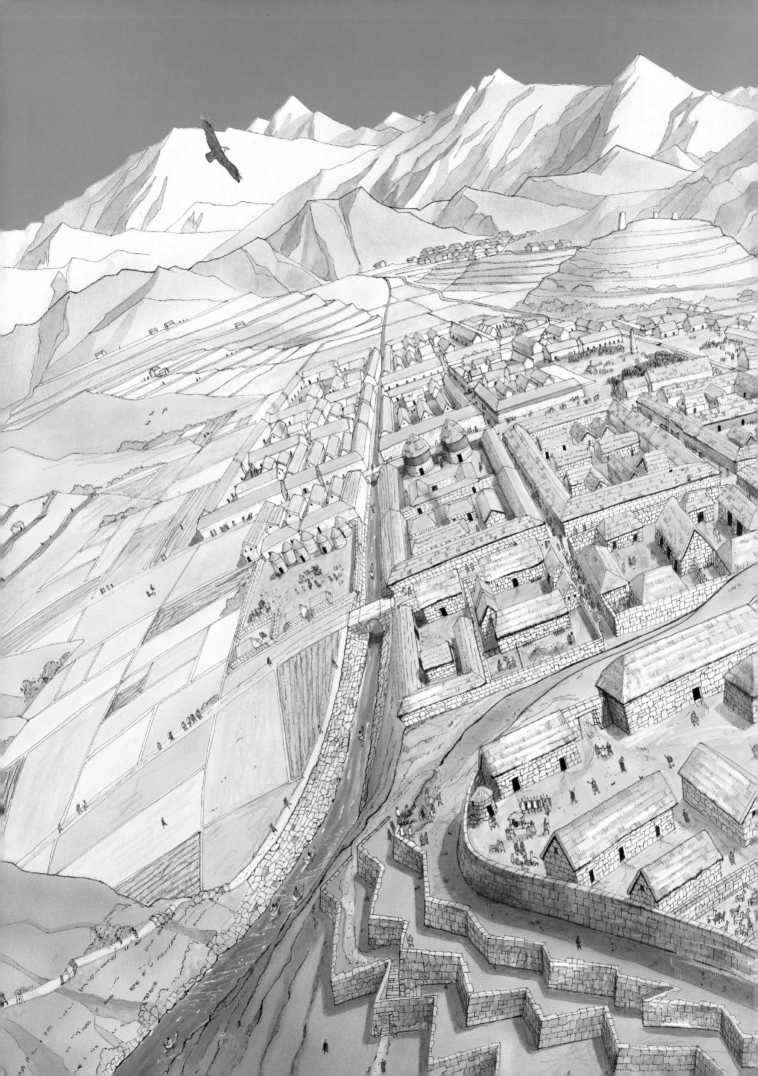